Preface:

This manuscript has been in the making for several years. It is a compilation of several of the messages that I have preached while I have ministered. I do not consider myself to be a writer by any means. It is with much reservation that I have even taken this to a publisher and set it into a book form. I do it not for its perfection of grammar, punctuation, or spelling, but because of its content may change a life.

If you could only see how I prepared my sermon notes in the beginning of my ministry and how I prepare them today. Quickly you would understand I have not had anyone teach me how this is done. I have set my notes up from the very beginning of my ministry, to be user friendly. If someone else would by chance ever get my notes to speak or preach from they could use them.

I have taken these prepared notes as my reference point to write this book. What I am actually doing is preaching my sermons through this media called a book. I hope that somewhere in this manuscript will be the words that will change someone's life. I hope that it will have an effect on everyone that takes time to read from these pages.

I was a forty-year-old man, with many problems in my own personal life when I surrendered to the Lord to preach. I hope the contents of this manuscript will help someone who is in a time of decision in their own life.

Please do not spend all your time looking over the errors of my writing, read the content.

I wish that I could give credit to everyone that has had any input in my ministry. I have read many books, pamphlets, and magazines during my lifetime. I have listen to my pastors preach, other preachers preach. I have listened to tapes, CD's and watched many Video's and DVD's. Yes, and by the way I do read and study the Bible. I do not know where every phrase in these chapters has been gleaned, but they are by no means my own and most are not even original. But, I will say the stories are mine and the format is mine and I have preached some of these messages over one hundred times in the past twenty years. I have no problem with you preaching from my book and even you calling it your own as long as you are pointing souls to Jesus Christ and His saving Grace.

In His Service,
Rodney Bankens

I am writing this manuscript from a burdened heart. As I have traveled extensively over the past twenty-six years of my life working in ministering the Word of God and finding so many Christian people that do not understand the message of New Testament salvation. This written manuscript I realize can be taken as a very controversial book for most Christian people today. This book is not written to discredit anyone or their walk and relationship with Jesus Christ.

I am a firm believer that the greatest event that will ever take place in someone's life is for him or her to make his or her calling an election sure by being born again. New Birth was spoken by Jesus Christ and also by the apostles that heard Him speak.

This New Birth experience is so much greater than many Christian people understand, and I have written this book in hopes of helping so many that have never experienced the Baptism of the Holy Ghost.

Let us all understand that Jesus Christ always responds to our efforts to draw closer to Him. As a young man I was taught that when we as humans take one step toward the Lord Jesus Christ He takes two steps towards us. Jesus Christ does respond to every one of us when we make a sincere effort to get ourselves near to Him.

I ask you to read this manuscript prayerfully and talk to Jesus as you read it and let Him show you His fulness.

Pastor Rodney Bankens

Philippians 2:12 KJV,
12 Wherefore, my beloved, as ye
have always obeyed, not as in my
presence only, but now much more in
my absence, work out your own
salvation with fear and trembling.

**Work Out Your Own Salvation with
Fear and Trembling**

"Was your salvation journey completed when you believed on Jesus Christ and committed your life to Him, or was this just the beginning?"

The road of Christian religion takes us down so many different paths, but we must not get hung up in Christian religion, but we must get to the point of our own personal salvation.

We must understand that men throughout the past generations have taken the written Word of God and manipulated it so that the simple message of salvation has become so confusing to those that are beginning their search and seeking to be near God. Men have incorrectly divided God's Holy Word by preaching scriptures out of context. Religious men have de-emphasized scriptures that point us all to our soul salvation while using scriptures that are directed to the church as scriptures of salvation. Therefore religious men have made the map to glory so different than the Bible states.

Ephesians 4:4-7 KJV,
4 There is one body, and one Spirit, even as ye are called in one hope of your calling;

5 One Lord, one faith, one baptism,

6 One God and Father of all, who is above all, and through all, and in you all.

7 But unto every one of us is given grace according to the measure of the gift of Christ.

We all understand that the Bible contains many mysteries and there are so many things that we may struggle to understand, but salvation is not a mystery, salvation is so very clear. This is the reason that we must open the written Word and search the scriptures in chronological order.

There is only one message of salvation in the Bible. I would like to use this opportunity to look at what the scripture has to say about salvation. Please take this manuscript with an open mind and heart as we together study the teachings of Jesus Christ and then follow the actions of

His disciples and followers after His ascension.

Each one of us has a personal responsibility when it comes to our salvation.

2 Peter 1:1-11 KJV,
1 Simon Peter, a servant and an apostle of Jesus Christ, to them that have obtained like precious faith with us through the righteousness of God and our Saviour Jesus Christ:

2 Grace and peace be multiplied unto you through the knowledge of God, and of Jesus our Lord,

3 According as his divine power hath given unto us all things that pertain unto life and godliness, through the knowledge of him that hath called us to glory and virtue:

4 Whereby are given unto us exceeding great and precious promises: that by these ye might be partakers of the divine nature, having escaped the corruption that is in the world through lust.

5 And beside this, giving all diligence, add to your faith virtue; and to virtue knowledge;

6 And to knowledge temperance; and to temperance patience; and to patience godliness;

7 And to godliness brotherly kindness; and to brotherly kindness charity.

8 For if these things be in you, and abound, they make you that ye shall neither be barren nor unfruitful in the knowledge of our Lord Jesus Christ.

9 But he that lacketh these things is blind, and cannot see afar off, and hath forgotten that he was purged from his old sins.

10 Wherefore the rather, brethren, give diligence to make your calling and election sure: for if ye do these things, ye shall never fall:

11 For so an entrance shall be ministered unto you abundantly into the everlasting kingdom of our Lord and Saviour Jesus Christ.

To we who are seeking salvation, giving diligence is the greatest need in our life.

Philippians 2:12 KJV,
12 Wherefore, my beloved, as ye have always obeyed, not as in my presence only, but now much more in my absence, work out your own salvation with fear and trembling.

For you and I as individuals we must lay aside any denominational bias and any handed down religious traditions or personal preconceptions and open the Word of God in deep study. We must Study the Word of God with an open mind and as the Word is openly revealed to us through the Spirit of God we can work out our salvation with the understanding that salvation is the most important thing we will ever strive for in our own personal lives.

One of the things that I have noticed as a minister of the gospel is that so many Christian people have never taken the assurance of their salvation to this level. It is sad to note that so many Christians have simply accepted passed down religious traditions or things that have been taught without comparing these teachings to the Word of God. So many Christians have never objectively explored the scriptures for themselves.

So many people have been raised in a certain denomination and have never studied the Word for themselves.

These folks are satisfied with what I like to call handed down family religious traditions. Then you have those that have joined a local church because they like the pastor, enjoyed the things they have felt or even been encouraged by the Word that they have heard preached. They have thereby accepted all that is presented as the plan of salvation and most of them do not even realize they must work out their own salvation with fear and with trembling.

The Bible does not teach us to accept those things that seem right good as the gospel.

Proverbs 16:25 KJV,
25 There is a way that seemeth right unto a man, but the end thereof are the ways of death.

We must make certain our salvation is completely scriptural and not a message that is religiously popular or politically correct. I realize it is not "religiously correct" in this day and hour to preach or teach the message of truth as strait as the Bible teaches.

Matthew 7:13-15 KJV,
13 Enter ye in at the strait gate: for wide is the gate, and broad is the way, that leadeth to destruction, and many there be which go in thereat:

14 Because strait is the gate, and narrow is the way, which leadeth unto life, and few there be that find it.

15 Beware of false prophets, which come to you in sheep's clothing, but inwardly they are ravening wolves.

There is something about this salvation Journey that takes us off the broad and puts us on a narrow path. We cannot follow the religious crowd or be moved to follow those who have taken the broad way. We must work out our salvation with fear and trembling. Yes we must give diligence to the greatest calling of our lives, which is to know we are saved according to His Word.

First, we must understand God has always had a plan. His plan has always been very specific. God has never offered multiple ways for people to get to Him. Even in this day and hour we can go all the way back to the beginning of His Word to understand this. God accepted Abel's offering but rejected Cain's offering. Cain was a tiller of the ground, a farmer. As a tiller of the ground Cain brought forth the fruit of the ground as His sacrifice to God. Cain brought a sacrifice to present that was important to him, something he had worked to produce. Yet, God rejected this sacrifice because it was not according to His divine plan.

According to human reasoning, the sacrifice that Cain brought forth should have sufficed, but it was not the sacrifice that God required. We

20

must understand as human beings we cannot rely on that which seems right and what seems to make sense to us we must follow the divine plan of God. We must each rely totally on that which has never changed and will never change, that is the Word of God.

When God told Noah He was going to destroy the world by flood, He gave him exact specifications on building the Ark. God did not give Noah a general concept to follow, but He gave Noah specific and detailed instructions to follow. We know that Noah worked hard for one hundred and twenty years and built the Ark as God had specified. When the rains came Noah and his family, of eight souls were saved from the floodwaters because Noah followed the divine plan of God.

When we study the Old Testament Tabernacle Plan, we find there was a certain order and specific directions for what the priest must do to roll the sins of the people forward.

There was a divine order that the priest had to follow and if they in any way tried to alter these plans they would not live. The priest of the Old Testament had to follow the specific and detail plans as God had them laid out for Him to fulfill.

The Bible plainly lets us know that our God has never changed and never will He change.

Hebrews 13:7-9 ESV,

7 Remember your leaders, those who spoke to you the word of God. Consider the outcome of their way of life, and imitate their faith.
8 Jesus Christ is the same yesterday and today and forever.
9 Do not be led away by diverse and strange teachings, for it is good for the heart to be strengthened by grace, not by foods, which have not benefited those devoted to them.

It is so sad to find that we see that in this generation of time Christianity is offering us a buffet or a pick and choose type of salvation, when the Word of God is so very clear and specific about His plan of salvation.

We must remember that everything that is built is built on a solid foundation. The foundation that I use in this manuscript is the very scriptures that will teach us how to study the Word of God.

2 Timothy 3:15-17 ESV,
15 and how from childhood you have been acquainted with the sacred writings, which are able to make you wise for salvation through faith in Christ Jesus.

16 All Scripture is breathed out by God and profitable for teaching, for reproof, for correction, and for training in righteousness,

17 that the man of God may be complete, equipped for every good work.

If we are to work out our salvation with fear and trembling and to make our calling and election sure, we must be certain that we take all scriptures that are related to salvation and to doctrine as foundational truth. We cannot just pick and choose only the scriptures we are familiar with or select just the scriptures that fall within our comfort zone and still be assured of our salvation. Thus our first step is that we must all understand the objective of Salvation is to take all scripture as it is written. Then secondly we must rightly divide the Word of God.

2 Timothy 2:14-15 KJV,
14 Of these things put them in remembrance, charging them before the Lord that they strive not about words to no profit, but to the subverting of the hearers.

15 Study to shew thyself approved unto God, a workman that needeth not to be ashamed, rightly dividing the word of truth.

In this scripture the Apostle Paul was instructing Timothy on the importance of correctly dividing the Word. Since the Apostle Paul spoke of a right way to divide the Word, obviously there must be a wrong way to divide the Word. Therefore, in order to rightly divide the Word we must explore for ourselves all that the Bible says about salvation with an awareness of the chronological order in which the events of the New Testament occurred.

The New Testament starts with the four gospels: Matthew, Mark, Luke and John. These four books record the life and times of Jesus Christ on this earth. In these four books we will also find the recorded Words of Jesus Christ. It is a must that we examine the Words that Jesus spoke and are recorded about salvation.

From the four gospels we must go to the next Book, which is Acts. I do not understand the reasoning of so many Christian people skipping over the Book of Acts; nor do I understand why so many denominational preachers refuse to preach from the Book of Acts. The Book of Acts is the recording of the beginning of the New Testament Church. In the Book of Acts we can find the things that Jesus Christ taught in the gospels being fulfilled.

As we have established our foundation of truth about salvation let us look in Hebrews.

Hebrews 2:1-4 KJV,

1Therefore we ought to give the more earnest heed to the things which we have heard, lest at any time we should let them slip.

2 For if the word spoken by angels was stedfast, and every transgression

and disobedience received a just recompence of reward;

3 How shall we escape, if we neglect so great salvation; which at the first began to be spoken by the Lord, and was confirmed unto us by them that heard him;

4 God also bearing them witness, both with signs and wonders, and with divers miracles, and gifts of the Holy Ghost, according to his own will?

In the third verse we see that the writer of Hebrews lays out the formula for this great salvation: First of all we see the fact that we will not be able to escape the destruction to come "if we neglect so great salvation." Secondly the writer expresses the fact that this great salvation was first spoken of by the Lord Jesus Christ Himself. The third fact we see in the writing of Hebrews is that those that heard Jesus speak also confirmed this great salvation to us. The only place that we can find this confirmation in writing is in the Book of Acts.

By deep study of the Book of Acts we find the formula for which the writer of Hebrews was confirming in Hebrews 2:3. In the Book of Acts we can see the fulfillment of all that was spoken by the Lord Jesus Christ Himself. In the Book of Acts we can follow those that heard Him and see that their preaching was confirmed with miracles, signs, wonders and multitudes being converted.

When we look objectively at what was first spoken by the Lord it is very important that we take all scripture that He spoke and not just one or two as the completed formula for salvation. So many want to establish John 3:16 as the formula for salvation, because Jesus spoke those Words.

John 3:16-19 NIV,
16 For God so loved the world that he gave his one and only Son, that whoever believes in him shall not perish but have eternal life.
17 For God did not send his Son into the world to condemn the world, but to save the world through him.

18 Whoever believes in him is not condemned, but whoever does not believe stands condemned already because they have not believed in the name of God's one and only Son. **19** This is the verdict: Light has come into the world, but people loved darkness instead of light because their deeds were evil.

While we do understand believing in Jesus Christ is very important, but believing alone is not salvation.

James 2:18-20 NLT,
18 Now someone may argue, "Some people have faith; others have good deeds." But I say, "How can you show me your faith if you don't have good deeds? I will show you my faith by my good deeds."

19 You say you have faith, for you believe that there is one God. Good for you! Even the demons believe this, and they tremble in terror.

20 How foolish! Can't you see that faith without good deeds is useless?

According to the writings of James, Even demons believe and tremble in terror, so by this we can see that believing alone does not save us. Jesus Christ has spoken about so much more than just believing. Once we have established and understood the Words that were spoken by Jesus we must also understand the Words that were recorded by those that heard Him. All of this should cause us to come to the place that we rightly divide the Word of God.

When we rightly divide the Word of God it is not like working a jigsaw puzzle. We are not to leave out certain scriptures. We are to simply let the scripture follow in chronological order so that the events unfold and reveal to us "so great salvation."

When we begin to study this subject of salvation, the logical thing to do is to examine the Words of Jesus Christ thoroughly. Many people make the statement they would rather read the Words of Jesus instead of just reading the Words of the apostles and followers. We must all understand and remember that now Jesus Christ is our Savior but one day Jesus Christ will be our judge and He will be the One to make sure that we fulfilled everything He spoke in His Word. We cannot be partially right or almost right we must be one hundred percent right in the things He proclaimed for us to do.

Matthew 16:15-19 KJV,

15 He saith unto them, But whom say ye that I am?

16 And Simon Peter answered and said, Thou art the Christ, the Son of the living God.

17 And Jesus answered and said unto him, Blessed art thou, Simon Barjona: for flesh and blood hath not revealed it unto thee, but my Father which is in heaven.

18 And I say also unto thee, That thou art Peter, and upon this rock I will build my church; and the gates of hell shall not prevail against it.

19 And **I will give unto thee the keys of the kingdom of heaven**: and whatsoever thou shalt bind on earth shall be bound in heaven: and whatsoever thou shalt loose on earth shall be loosed in heaven.

In verse 19, Jesus placed an amazing amount of trust in the Apostle Peter. This scripture is very critical in our search of salvation. Because Peter understood who Jesus Christ was, Jesus gave Him the Keys to the Kingdom of Heaven. This was not a literal set of Keys but these keys are the literal words that Peter would speak. Jesus was telling Peter whatever you bind and whatever you loose will be backed by the Kingdom of Heaven. If we desire to be part of the Kingdom of Heaven, wouldn't it make sense that we follow the message of the man who had been given the Keys to unlock the doors to salvation in the early church? We must follow the words of peter when we are seeking and searching out our salvation. Peter was the one that Jesus Christ Himself trusted to show us the way. We will see by following the words of Peter, there were no contradictions in His message and the Words of Jesus Christ. Peter's words were only an incredible confirmation to all that Jesus had spoken.

Jesus told us: **Mark 16:15-16 KJV,**
15 And he said unto them, Go ye into
all the world, and preach the gospel
to every creature.

16 He that believeth and is baptized
shall be saved; but he that believeth
not shall be damned.

The Words spoken by Jesus is tying
two things to salvation: we must
believe and we must be baptized.
Since Jesus used the conjunction and,
can we just pick and choose one of
the two and say like so many
Christian people that believing is all
we have to do. So many Christian
teachers and preachers do not
preach that baptism is essential to

38

salvation. They say that baptism is a good thing, but is not necessary for salvation. So many Christians have been taught that baptism is just an outward sign of an inward heart. Jesus presents believing and baptism as equally important. The Bible is so plain and teaches us the fact that baptism is absolutely necessary for our salvation. In fact not only is baptism essential for our salvation, but there is a specific formula and a specific purpose for baptism that is recorded in the Book of Acts.

Along with believing and baptism, in scripture Jesus points us to Jerusalem where two elements of our salvation where to be preached: repentance and remission of sins.

Luke 24:45-47 KJV,
45 Then opened he their understanding, that they might understand the scriptures,

46 And said unto them, Thus it is written, and thus it behooved Christ to suffer, and to rise from the dead the third day:

47 And that repentance and remission of sins should be preached in his name among all nations, beginning at Jerusalem.

At the very core of our salvation experience our sins must be dealt with. We must repent and then our sins must be remitted through baptism in the Name of Jesus Christ for the remission of our sins, this is critical. The fact that Jesus tells us in His Word, that repentance and remission should be preached in His name beginning in Jerusalem is a point that should not be overlooked.

When we understand that Jesus Christ died on the old rugged cross, He was buried in a borrowed tomb and on the third day He arose with victory. In like manner you and I must repent, in similarity we must lay ourselves on the altar of sacrifice and die out to sin through repentance. Once anything dies it must be buried, so in like manner once we repent and die at the altar of sacrifice we must be buried in baptism in the name of Jesus Christ for the remission of sins. Then as Jesus arose from the grave we are raised from the water grave of

41

baptism and we come forth with victory by receiving the baptism of the Holy Spirit.

Jesus told the disciples in **John 7:38-39 KJV,**

> **38** He that believeth on me, as the scripture hath said, out of his belly shall flow rivers of living water.

> **39** (But this spake he of the Spirit, which they that believe on him should receive: for the Holy Ghost was not yet given; because that Jesus was not yet glorified.)

Jesus teaches that when we believe according to scripture, we should receive the Holy Ghost. The problem with a common but faulty interpretation of salvation lies in the fact that many Christian people try to skip around the necessity of receiving the baptism of the Holy Ghost. So many Christians are aligning themselves with only certain scriptures while they negate the many scriptures that point us to so great salvation.

Paul wrote, 2 Timothy 3:15-17 KJV,

15 And that from a child thou hast known the holy scriptures, which are able to make thee wise unto salvation through faith which is in Christ Jesus.

16 All scripture is given by inspiration of God, and is profitable for doctrine, for reproof, for correction, for instruction in righteousness:

17 That the man of God may be perfect, thoroughly furnished unto all good works.

When we incorporate all scripture, we start the process by believing on Jesus Christ as the scripture has said then we will receive the Holy Ghost or the promise from on high. The Holy Ghost is the promise that Jesus Christ called the comforter that He would send to those that believed.

We have viewed the foundational truth of this great truth of salvation. We have viewed what was spoken first by the Lord Himself. We will now view the scriptures written and recorded by those who heard him and confirmed all that He had spoken. Let us continue to rightly divide the Word of God and follow it in the order the events as they occurred and not jumped from place to place as though salvation is a jigsaw puzzle that we struggle to put together.

We will now go into the very next book of the Bible, which is the most neglected book preached in Christianity, the Book of Acts, where the church begins.

Acts 1:3-4 KJV,

3 To whom also he shewed himself alive after his passion by many infallible proofs, being seen of them forty days, and speaking of the things pertaining to the kingdom of God:

4 And, being assembled together with them, commanded them that they should not depart from Jerusalem, but wait for the promise of the Father, which, saith he, ye have heard of me.

Jesus had just spent forty days after His resurrection speaking to His disciples of things pertaining to the kingdom of God. After this forty days of intense teaching with Jesus Christ the resurrected savior. I realize by reading the scripture that these disciples heard Him well, as we will see as we progress through the scriptures. What we see happening in the next few chapters is exactly what the Lord Himself had in mind. We must remember,

Hebrews 2:3 KJV,

3 How shall we escape, if we neglect so great salvation; which at the first began to be spoken by the Lord, and was confirmed unto us by them that heard him;

We must realize that these disciples are the same ones that heard Jesus teach and recorded the truths they had heard Him speak.

Acts 1:8-9 KJV,

8 But ye shall receive power, after that the Holy Ghost is come upon you: and ye shall be witnesses unto me both in Jerusalem, and in all Judaea, and in Samaria, and unto the uttermost part of the earth.

9 And when he had spoken these things, while they beheld, he was taken up; and a cloud received him out of their sight.

Now for the first time, everything that Jesus Christ lived for and died for is ready to be fulfilled.

Acts 1:10-12 KJV,
10 And while they looked stedfastly toward heaven as he went up, behold, two men stood by them in white apparel;

11 Which also said, Ye men of Galilee, why stand ye gazing up into heaven? this same Jesus, which is taken up from you into heaven, shall so come in like manner as ye have seen him go into heaven.

12 Then returned they unto Jerusalem from the mount called Olivet, which is from Jerusalem a sabbath day's journey.

The disciples along with other followers returned to Jerusalem. Remember this is the city that Jesus told His disciples that remissions of sin would begin in Jerusalem.

Luke 24:47 KJV,

47 And that repentance and remission of sins should be preached in his name among all nations, beginning at Jerusalem.

Now if the disciples wanted to follow His message correctly, they had to go

49

back to the place Jesus said it would begin. We see in the scripture the disciples and His followers went back to Jerusalem. They gathered in the upper room to wait for the promise that Jesus told them was going to come. On the day of Pentecost the Holy Ghost falls upon each and every one of them and they all began to speak with other tongues as the Spirit gave them utterance.

Acts 2:1-4 KJV,
2 And when the day of Pentecost was fully come, they were all with one accord in one place.

2 And suddenly there came a sound from heaven as of a rushing mighty wind, and it filled all the house where they were sitting.

3 And there appeared unto them cloven tongues like as of fire, and it sat upon each of them.

4 And they were all filled with the Holy Ghost, and began to speak with other tongues, as the Spirit gave them utterance.

As we focus on this phenomenon we see that multitudes of people that are in Jerusalem celebrating the Feast of Pentecost are drawn to the noise that is coming from the 120 in the upper room. When they came to where the disciples and followers of Jesus were these Jews noticed something strange was going on within the crowd.

Acts 2:12-13 KJV,

12 And they were all amazed, and were in doubt, saying one to another, What meaneth this?

13 Others mocking said, These men are full of new wine.

We must understand in the first portion of the Book of Acts takes place among the Jews. So those who were mocking the phenomenon that was taking place in the upper room on the Day of Pentecost were not followers of Jesus, nor were they believers. Jesus had taught that we must believe in order for us to be saved. Let us to a quick review of the elements so that we have the whole picture in our mind.

After Jesus resurrection, He spent forty days teaching and talking with His disciples. He then ascended up to glory, after which the disciples and some of the followers returned to the upper room in Jerusalem. Now they were assembled together in one accord in the upper room and when the Day of Pentecost was fully come they were all filled with the Holy Ghost and this great phenomenon drew a multitude of unbeliever's and they were all amazed with marvel and many of them begin to question as other mocked. How can this be are not all these that we hear speaking from Galilee? The mockers had a quick answer, "These men are all drunk."

Notice in scripture it was Peter that stepped up and preached to the scoffers and unbelievers.

Acts 2:14-16 KJV,

14 But Peter, standing up with the eleven, lifted up his voice, and said unto them, Ye men of Judaea, and all ye that dwell at Jerusalem, be this known unto you, and hearken to my words:

15 For these are not drunken, as ye suppose, seeing it is but the third hour of the day.

16 But this is that which was spoken by the prophet Joel;

Peter begins to preach to these bewildered Jews in Acts 2:14-36 but notice what happens in verse 37 as

Peter comes to the close of his message.

Acts 2:37 KJV,

37 Now when they heard this, they were pricked in their heart, and said unto Peter and to the rest of the apostles, Men and brethren, what shall we do?

We see that Peter has now preached such a convicting message that the doubters and mockers have been moved from unbelief to the point of believing. These Jews were no longer mocking but were instead asking Peter what it was that they needed to do to receive the Holy Ghost? The scriptures have so vividly stated that they that heard the Words of Jesus would confirm this great salvation. Now the Jews in Jerusalem on the Day of Pentecost were asking Peter and the rest of the apostles, these are the ones who had been with Jesus and heard Him speak, "Men and brethren what shall we do?" Remember, Peter and the apostles were Jews just like those that were in question. For the first time since Jesus had ascended salvation is being preached to this lost world.

There are so many Christian people, preachers included who skip around this portion of scripture, and many even claim it is not for this day and hour. **To skip this portion of God's Word is not rightly dividing the**

Word of God and dooming
multitudes of honest hearted
people to hell. This is the beginning
of the New Testament Church that
Jesus Himself suffered, bled and
died to establish upon this earth.

Peter, the man with the keys to the
kingdom presents to them the plan
of salvation. This is a fulfillment of
the Words spoken by Jesus Christ
Himself.

Acts 2:38 KJV,

38 Then Peter said unto them,
Repent, and be baptized every one
of you in the name of Jesus Christ
for the remission of sins, and ye

shall receive the gift of the Holy Ghost.

Peter is giving them the answer to the question of "what shall we do?" The three steps that Peter gave them fulfilled the Words spoken by Jesus Christ Himself.

1) Repentance (Luke 24:47)

2) Baptism (Mark 16:16) and in Jesus Name for the remission of sins (Luke 24:47)

3) Receiving the Holy Ghost (John 7:38)

Let us recall what the writer of Hebrews says:

Hebrews 2:3 KJV,

3 How shall we escape, if we neglect so great salvation; which at the first began to be spoken by the Lord, and was confirmed unto us by them that heard him;

Repentance was spoken by the Lord in Luke 24:47, was confirmed by Peter (one who heard Him) in Acts 2:38.

Baptism was spoken by the Lord in Mark 16:16, was confirmed by Peter (one who heard Him) Acts 2:38.

Remission of sins in His Name in Luke 24:47, was confirmed by Peter (one who heard Him) In the Name of Jesus Christ for the remission of sins Acts 2:38.

As we begin to see in the Book of Acts, Peter the man with the keys to the kingdom fulfills everything as he had heard Jesus speak it. When we rightly divide the Word of God and begin to search the scripture with a hungry and pure heart we will come to the conclusion that Acts 2:38 is the only formula for salvation.

But remember when you have followed the Words of Jesus Christ and the apostles you will have found for yourself "A New Beginning" there is so much more for you.

"Work Out Your Own Salvation with Fear and Trembling."

Made in the USA
Las Vegas, NV
15 March 2022

45417251R00036